Myths Behind Words

Myths
Behind
Words

GREEK MYTHOLOGY
IN ENGLISH WORDS AND EXPRESSIONS

Compiled by
Alexander Zaphiriou

AIORA

Cover artwork and illustrations by Panagiotis Stavropoulos

First edition April 2018
Reprinted April 2019

ISBN: 978-618-5048-89-1

AIORA PRESS
11 Mavromichali St.
Athens 10679 – Greece
tel: +30 210 3839000
www.aiora.gr
www.aiorabooks.com

Contents

Introduction

One of the reasons for language being such a fascinating subject is precisely the trajectories that words are seen to inscribe across time, as if they had embarked on a pilgrimage or a quest, before arriving to alight on the lips of the people who speak them. Roughly one in twenty words in the English language are of Greek provenance. Of those, a noteworthy, albeit very small, subset comprises words or expressions that are rooted in Greek myth and preserve a meaningful kinship to the mythological narratives from which they emerged before gaining currency in English. This compilation aims to gather them all in a single volume.

Cosmogony

At the beginning of all existence arose
the formless void, Chaos, from which
came the Earth, the Sky, the Night and
all the primordial gods. From them
were born the elder gods and first
divine rulers, the Titans,
and the Giants.

Chaotic

Utter disorder, inchoate.

The word Chaos [χάος] comes from χαίνω (gape) and χάσμα (chasm) and indicates a primordial nothingness from which all else sprang. She, for Chaos is feminine, also stands for the lower atmosphere that surrounds the Earth, holding it apart from the sky. This concept has a parallel in Genesis 1:1–2, 'In the beginning God created the heaven and the earth. And the earth was without form, and void; and darkness was upon the face of the deep.'

Ethereal

Delicate and otherworldly.

Aether [αιθήρ] was a primordial deity personifying the sublime air breathed by the gods, in contrast to the inferior air [αήρ], breathed by humanity.

Titanic

Mighty and immense.

The Titans were the original race of ruling gods, the six sons and six daughters of Uranus [Ουρανός] (Sky) and Gaea [Γαία] (Earth). The twelve Olympian gods, off-spring of the Titans Cronus and Rhea, fought against them for supremacy in a war that became known as the Titanomachy, and ultimately succeeded in hurling them from Olympus into the nether darkness beneath Tartarus, the deepest part of Hades.

Ocean

A very large expanse of sea.

The Titan Oceanus [Ὠκεανός], eldest son of Uranus and Gaea, was a great river encircling the mass of dry land that constituted the Earth. In most versions of the Titanomachy, Oceanus withdrew from the conflict along with the Titaness Themis and her son Prometheus. He had also earlier refused to side with his brother Cronus in the latter's revolt against their father, Uranus.

Atlantic

One of the earth's oceans.

The Atlantic derives its name from the Titan Atlas, who, as punishment for fighting against the Olympians in the Titanomachy, was condemned to bear the sky upon his shoulders. It was thought that he stood and held the sky from a point near the Straits of Hercules (Gibraltar). He was petrified by the Gorgon's head and his stony body formed the Atlas Mountain Range across North Africa.

Typhoon

Hurricane.

Typhon [Τυφών] was the son of Gaea and Tartarus, whom Gaea begat to avenge herself on the Olympian gods for having overthrown the Titans. The poet Hesiod says:

Strength was with his hands in all that he did and the feet of the strong god were untiring. From his shoulders grew a hundred heads of a snake, a fearful dragon, with dark, flickering tongues, and from under the brows of his eyes in his marvelous heads flashed fire, and fire burned from his heads as he glared. And there were voices in all his dreadful heads which uttered every kind of sound unspeakable; for at one time they made sounds such that the gods understood, but at another, the noise of a bull bellowing aloud in proud ungovernable fury; and at another, the sound of a lion, relentless of heart; and at another, sounds like whelps, wonderful to hear; and again, at another, he would hiss, so that the mountains re-echoed.[1]

Promethean

*Daringly original
in inventiveness
and creativity,
rule-breaking.*

Prometheus, son of the Titans Iapetus and
Themis, was the inventor of many arts,
and is said to have made man from clay.
Taking pity on benighted mankind,
Prometheus brought man the gifts of art-
ful wisdom and fire, stolen from Athena
and Hephaestus respectively: hence his
name means 'forethought', in contrast to
that of his careless brother Epimetheus,
meaning 'afterthought'. Zeus punished
Prometheus for his audacity, and had him
shackled to a rock on Mount Caucasus by
the smith-god Hephaestus. There, an eagle
would visit him every day, tear through his
flesh and eat his liver, which would regen-
erate overnight—for Prometheus was im-

Prometheus: Detail from a black-figured clay kylix,
about 550 BCE, Vatican Museums, Rome.

mortal—and perpetuate the agony. Hercules, on his way to fetch the golden apples of the Hesperides, his eleventh labour, killed the eagle and broke Hephaestus' chains, delivering Prometheus from his torment.

Pandora's Box

*Something broached in ignorance
of its dire consequences.*

The box—which, strictly speaking, was not a box but an earthenware jar—was the dowry of Pandora ('all gifts'), the wife given to Epimetheus by the gods. She had been commanded to leave it untouched but her curiosity got the better of her and she opened it to see inside, thus setting loose all the woes and afflictions that beset mankind. Only Hope could not fly away, for Pandora managed to slam the lid shut in time.

Immortals

The twelve major Olympian gods were
Zeus, Hera, Ares, Aphrodite, Apollo,
Artemis, Athena, Demeter, Dionysus,
Hephaestus, Hermes, Hestia (before
yielding her place to Dionysus) and
Poseidon. They resided on Mount
Olympus in central Greece.
The Olympians as well as many other
minor deities of the Greek Pantheon
impacted the lives of mortals
to support or persecute them.

Olympian

*Imperturbable, beyond the toil
and anguish of the world.*

The reference is to Greece's tallest mountain, Mount Olympus, as the home of the immortal gods who had none of the cares of mortal beings.

Erotic

*Anything pertaining to the craving
of sexual love.*

Eros sprang straight from Chaos and is
thus a primordial god who presides over
loving desire, causing his victims to fall in
love even in spite of themselves. The irre-
sistible attraction he generates between
lovers guarantees their procreation. In
Hesiod's telling, he was the third god to
come into existence, along with Gaea and
Tartarus.

Athenaeum

Used to name libraries, scientific and literary institutions, and relevant publications.

The first such institution was a famous school for the promotion of literary and scientific studies. It was founded in Rome by the emperor Hadrian, who was enamoured of philosophy and of what he regarded as philosophy's birthplace, the city of Athens, whose patron deity was Athena, goddess of wisdom.

Arachnid

*Denoting the class of eight-legged
arthropods known as spiders.*

Arachne was a beautiful mortal maiden
who provoked Athena's jealousy for having mastered the craft of weaving to per-
fection, causing the goddess to change her
into a spider.

Gorgon Stare

*A look so grim and fierce
it could turn those who looked
upon it to stone.*

The Gorgons were three sisters, monsters with snakes for hair, huge staring eyes, and fangs for teeth. One of the three, Medusa, was mortal. She was beheaded by the demi-god hero Perseus, who then presented her head to Athena. The goddess affixed it to her shield, the Aegis, and gave it to Zeus.

Under the Aegis

*Under the auspices, i.e. under
a benevolent, protective power.*

The aegis was the shield borne by both
Athena and Zeus. The shield was made
from the skin of the goat Amalthea, who
had nurtured the infant Zeus and whose
horn was the cornucopia, the horn of
plenty. On the aegis was attached the head
of Medusa, offered by Perseus as a trophy
to the goddess Athena.

Apollonian

Ruled by reason
and calm.

Apollo was the god of measured and gracious expression, music and poetry, among many other things. The apollonian, therefore, is in opposition to thedionysian, which refers to Dionysus, the god of revelry, and denotes the frenzied and ecstatic.

Museum

*A place dedicated
to the study of the arts.*

The nine Muses ministered to the arts,
under Apollo's lead, serving as sources of
inspiration: Calliope ('beautiful-voiced')
to epic poetry, Clio ('making famous') to
history, Euterpe ('delightful') to lyric poetry and the flute, Thalia ('flourishing') to
comedy and pastoral poetry, Melpomene
('melodius') to tragedy, Terpsichore ('de-
lighting in dance') to dance, Erato ('desir-
able') to love poetry, Polyhymnia ('of
many praises') to sacred poetry, and Ura-
nia ('heavenly') to astronomy. Museums
were temples dedicated to the Muses,
the first considered to have been the one
of Plato in Athens. Another was the
Musaeum of Alexandria founded by
Ptolemy I Soter c. 280 BCE, which pro-
moted philosophy and research.

Dionysian

Uninhibited, frenzied.

Dionysus, god of wine, ecstasy, and frenzied celebration, was the winter double of Apollo's summer glory and instructed his followers on how to be (temporarily) freed of their inhibitions.

Bacchanal

Orgiastic celebration.

Bacchus is another name of Dionysus that refers specifically to a loosening of propriety and reserve, with the help of wine and ecstatic dance, hence the conceptual link between bacchanals and orgies.

Hermeneutic

Regarding interpretation.

As divine messenger, Hermes was patron of eloquence, and of commerce and road travel, as well as of lies and thieving. Among his numerous inventions were the alphabet, music, numbers, measures, weights, astronomy, gymnastics, and the art of fighting. 'Hermeneutics' in its early usage belonged within the ambit of the sacred. Messages from the gods, in their ambiguity, posed an implicit quandary. Hermes delighted in the unease of the addressees of the messages he delivered. As a technical term, 'hermeneía' was introduced by Aristotle c. 360 BCE, in his *On Interpretation*, among the earliest Western philosophical texts on the relationship between language and logic.

Hermetic

Secret, concealed, occult, airtight.

For Greeks in Hellenistic Egypt, Hermes became conflated with the Egyptian god Thoth, as both were psychopomps (conductors of souls to the Underworld), and the two were worshiped as one in the temple at Khemnu. Thoth/Hermes was deemed the true author of everything discovered and generated by the human mind, the father of all wisdom, law, worship, and sundry inventions, and was therefore named 'thrice great': Trismegistus. In the early centuries CE, he became central to a quasi-religious movement, akin to neo-Pythagoreanism. The movement's writings, the *Corpus Hermeticum*, comprised multitudes of highly venerated texts. 'Hermetic' thus refers to Trismegistus and the magic seal he invented to keep the occult texts secret.

Aphrodisiac

Substances, ideas or things that induce sexual arousal.

Aphrodite, the goddess of allure, beauty, and sexual craving, bestows her name to aphrodisiacs and things that breed desire. To keep the gods from fighting over her, she was made to marry Hephaestus, the deformed, ugly god of fire, metalworking and craftsmanship. Nevertheless, she famously had affairs with Ares, Poseidon, Hermes, Dionysus, Zeus and Adonis, as well as with three mortals, Phaethon, Anchises and Butes.

Hermaphrodite

Simultaneously male and female.

Hermaphroditus was the child of the union of Hermes and Aphrodite, and bore the sexual attributes of both deities. According to Diodorus Siculus:

[Hermaphroditus] was born with a physical body which is a combination of that of a man and that of a woman, in that he has a body which is beautiful and delicate like that of a woman, but has the masculine quality and vigour of a man. But there are some who declare that such creatures of two sexes are monstrosities, and coming rarely into the world as they do they have the quality of presaging the future, sometimes for evil and some times for good.[2]

Ambrosial

Delicious and fragrant.

Ambrosia [Αμβροσία] was the food of the gods of Olympus, and bestowed immortality. The word arises from βροτός meaning 'mortal', preceded by a privative 'α', thus 'immortal'.

Nectar

Sweet liquid in flowers,
made into honey by bees.

Nectar was the delectable drink of the gods of Olympus, and, like ambrosia, bestowed immortality. It accompanied all Olympian feasts, and was initially served to the gods by Hebe, daughter of Zeus and Hera (whose name forms the root of the word 'ephebe', meaning 'adolescent'), and subsequently by Ganymede, the cupbearer and favourite of Zeus.

Aeolian Harp

*A musical instrument suspended
from the boughs of trees, producing
sounds as the wind wafts
through its strings.*

The god Aeolus was 'the keeper of the winds', which he would confine in a bag or release at Zeus's bidding. Wind chimes follow the same principle as aeolian harps.

Morphine

*An opioid that induces sleep
and acts as a painkiller, derived
from poppy juice extract.*

Morphine is named for Morpheus, a god of dreams and sleep. He was a sibling or son of Hypnos [Ὕπνος] (Sleep), and therefore Nyx [Νύξ] (Night), the latter's mother, was either Morpheus's mother or grandmother.

Protean

Changing shape.

Proteus was a shape-shifting god of the seas and rivers who, so long as he could not be pinned down, would evade those who sought his counsel. In the *Odyssey*, Proteus is captured by Menelaus while coming ashore for the night to sleep among his colony of seals. Although Proteus changes into many shapes, Menelaus manages to keep hold of him, thereby forcing Proteus to reveal several important pieces of information, including that Odysseus was being held captive on the island of Calypso. The *Amoeba proteus*, one of the most common species of amoebas, is named after the god, describing the pseudopods which make them seem to change shape continually.

Hygiene

*Practices that preserve and
safeguard health.*

Hygeia, the goddess of health, and specifically of the prevention of disease, was the daughter of Asclepius, the god of medicine. Her name was enshrined in the concept of healthiness and the habits that promote it.

Iridescent

Changing colour along the visible spectrum from red to violet, depending on how the light falls.

As a messenger of the gods, Iris was a personification of the rainbow, an emblem of the gods' communication with mortals. Her name is therefore appropriate to describe the phenomenon that makes certain surfaces appear to shimmer and change colour as the angle of observation or illumination changes.

Panic

Sudden and uncontrollable fear.

Pan, with his goat legs, cloven hooves and horned brow, was the god of the wild, shepherds and flocks, forests and rustic music. He was variously held to be the son of Hermes, Zeus or Dionysus. His fearsome aspect may be the reason he was supposed to inspire the overwhelming terror we call panic.

Priapism

A state of perpetual sexual arousal.

As a god of fertility, livestock, sex and masculinity, Priapus was depicted with a permanently engorged phallus. His name has therefore come to describe the condition in which men are in a state of continual tumescence.

Adonis

A beautiful young male.

The god Adonis was emblematic of spring, which lives, dies and is reborn every year. The god was typically portrayed as a youthful and beautiful divinity of vegetation. He was one of the lovers of Aphrodite and when he was gored by a bull and lay dying in her arms, where droplets of her tears mingled with his blood fell to the ground, anemones sprouted.

Hubris

Excessive arrogance or overweening pride.

Hubris described the flouting of behavioural norms, of violations of honour and, specifically, of mortals vying with the gods through acts of pride or overconfidence. Ineluctably, such behaviour would attract Nemesis, the goddess of retribution and the downfall of the one indulging in hubris. Those punished for hubris included Arachne, Niobe and Icarus, who was given wings constructed of wax and feather by his father, Daedalus. Ignoring his father's admonitions not to fly too high and close to the sun, the wings melted and Icarus fell into the sea and drowned.

Nemesis

Retribution, comeuppance.

Nemesis, the goddess of retribution, personified the resentment of the gods, in retaliation to a violation of proper bounds. She had the responsibility to distribute to every mortal that which was due to him or her, meting out punishment and destroying the happiness of those who had achieved it without earning it. Her interventions were regarded as a matter of fairness that would not allow acts of hubris to go unpunished.

Narcissism

A fixation with one's self and appearance or public image.

Narcissus, a hunter from Boeotia, was beautiful and proud, paying no heed to those who loved him. When the goddess Nemesis saw his behaviour, she brought Narcissus to a pool of water. Noticing his visage mirrored in the surface of the water, he immediately fell in love with it—not realizing it to be only an image—and could not bring himself to part from it. Losing his will to live, he gazed at his reflection until he died.

Echo

Reverberated sound.

Echo was a nymph of the kind that Zeus was fond of consorting with. Her suspicions aroused, Hera, Zeus's wife, tried to catch her husband in the act. Echo, in her effort to shield Zeus, incurred the wrath of the goddess, who deprived her of the power of speech, except to repeat the last few words spoken to her. When Echo saw Narcissus at the pool and fell in love with him, she was unable to speak to him of her feelings, and had to watch him as he lay dying of his unrequited love for himself, her own love equally unrequited.

Argus-eyed

Ever vigilant and watchful.

Argus Panoptes ('all-seeing') was a many-eyed giant who was set by Hera the task of keeping watch over the nymph Io, tethered and in the form of a heifer, and one of Hera's rivals for Zeus's attentions. At Zeus's behest, so that Io might go free, Hermes slew Argus, then handed the giant's eyes over to Hera, who used them to adorn the tails of the peacocks that pulled her carriage.

Halcyon Days

*Bright interval in adversity,
or a formerly glorious time.
Alternately, unseasonal
balmy weather.*

Alcyone, daughter of Aeolus, and her husband, Ceyx, would often address each other as 'Zeus' and 'Hera' in their insouciance. When Zeus's anger at their hubris caused their deaths, the gods took pity on them, changing them both into halcyons, that is, kingfishers. Halcyon days therefore are the fourteen days in winter in the Mediterranean when storms are made to abate by Aeolus, so that the birds can come on shore to build their nests and lay their eggs.

Sorrows
or Tears of Niobe

*A mother's bereavement for
the loss of her children.*

A daughter of Tantalus who, having
boasted of her many children to Leto, was
punished for her hubris by Leto's twins,
Apollo and Artemis, who slayed Niobe's
children with their arrows. Niobe's dead
children lay unburied for nine days while
she abstained from food; on the tenth, the
gods buried them themselves. Niobe is
named in Homer's *Iliad* when grieving
King Priam visits Achilles to request Hec-
tor's body and he is urged by the hero to
break his fast:

Even lovely Niobe had to think about eating,
though her twelve children—six daughters
and six lusty sons—had been all slain in her
house. Apollo killed the sons with arrows
from his silver bow, to punish Niobe, and

Artemis slew the daughters, because Niobe had vaunted herself against Leto; she said Leto had borne two children only, whereas she had herself borne many—whereon the two killed the many. Nine days did they lie weltering, and there was none to bury them, for the son of Cronos turned the people into stone; but on the tenth day the gods in heaven themselves buried them, and Niobe then took food, being worn out with weeping. They say that somewhere among the rocks on the mountain pastures of Sipylus, where the nymphs live that haunt the river Achelous, there she lives in stone and still nurses the sorrows sent upon her by the hand of heaven.[3]

Europe

One of the Earth's continents.

Europa [Ευρώπη] ('wide faced') was a beautiful Phoenician princess, seduced and abducted by Zeus in the form of a bull, and brought on the bull's back to Crete. The European continent is named after her. The term 'Europa' is first used in a geographic sense in the Homeric 'Hymn to Delian Apollo' in reference to the western shore of the Aegean Sea. As a name for a part of the known world, it was first used by the pre-Socratic philosopher Anaximander, and the historian and geographer Hecataeus in the sixth century BCE.

Europa and the Bull: Detail from a red-figured kylix,
about 330–320 BCE, Kunsthistorisches Museum, Vienna.

Danaids' Sieve

*Instrument of a futile task
or wasteful practice.*

The fifty daughters of Danaus were to marry the fifty sons of Aegyptus, Danaus's brother. On their wedding night, at Danaus's bidding, they all killed their husbands, save one, and so were doomed to spend eternity filling a perforated jar with water. The single exception was Hypermnestra, who spared Lynceus because he had respected her wish to remain a virgin.

Midas Touch

*The knack of turning one's
undertakings to significant profit.*

King Midas was granted his wish to have everything he touched turn into gold. But when he realized that this would also happen to his food and to his loved ones, he prayed to Dionysus (who had granted his wish in the first place) to be released from this bane. The god heeded his prayer and instructed Midas to wash in the river Pactolus, so that his power should flow into the river. As a result, the river's sands became rich in gold, and still today its name, in Greek, is synonymous with an inexhaustible source of wealth.

Hades

The Underworld is the domain of the shades of the dead, ruled over by Hades (also known as Pluton), Zeus's brother. Upon the defeat of the Titans, the sons of Cronus cast lots for their domains: Zeus got the Upper World, Poseidon the Sea, and Hades the Netherworld.

Descent into Hades

The harrowing of Hell.

When the word 'Hades' is used to describe hell or the underworld, the reference is to the ancient Greek realm of the dead. The theological term for the period between Christ's Crucifixion and the Resurrection is still described in the Orthodox Christian tradition as Christ's 'descent into Hades'. In Greek mythology, a hero or deity visits the netherworld and returns with a thing or person, or with special knowledge, as did Orpheus (to regain Euridice), Hercules (to fetch Cerberus and release Theseus, then again to fetch Alcestis), Theseus (to help Pirithous abduct Persephone), and Odysseus (to consult Tiresias).

Orphic

*Initiated or pertaining
to Orphism, things that are
mystical or entrancing.*

Orpheus was a musician of such skill he could tame wild beasts with his song. To him are attributed certain religious beliefs and practices found in Ancient Greece and the Hellenistic world, as well as in Thrace, that revered Persephone (who went down to Hades every winter and returned in spring) and Dionysus (who had also been to Hades and returned). Initiation into the Orphic Mysteries vouchsafed benefits in the afterlife, just as the Eleusinian Mysteries did.

Sop to Cerberus

*An inducement given
to allay trouble.*

Cerberus, the offspring of Echidna and Typhon, was the three-headed, serpent-tailed dog guarding Hades. Visitors to the underworld would offer him honey-cakes—sops—to bypass him. Capturing Cerberus was Hercules' twelfth and last labour.

Hercules and Cerberus: Detail from a black-figured
clay hydria, about 525 BCE, Louvre, Paris.

Sisyphean Task

Unending and futile hard labour.

Sisyphus was set to perform a pointless, never-ending task in Hades as punishment for killing guests, thus violating Zeus's law of hospitality, and also for cheating Death, when he tricked Charon into putting himself in chains to demonstrate how the dead were chained while ferried to the Underworld. In the *Odyssey*, Odysseus describes his torment thus:

And I saw Sisyphus at his endless task raising his prodigious stone with both his hands. With hands and feet he tried to roll it up to the top of the hill, but always, just before he could roll it over on to the other side, its weight would be too much for him, and the pitiless stone would come thundering down again on to the plain. Then he would begin trying to push it up hill again, and the sweat ran off him and the steam rose after him.[4]

Tantalizing

*Desired yet always
just out of reach.*

Tantalus, a mortal son of Zeus, dined with him and stole ambrosia and nectar to bring back to his people. He also had his own son cut in pieces, boiled, and served to the gods. For this, he was punished to perpetual hunger and thirst, which in the *Odyssey* Odysseus describes as:

I saw also the dreadful fate of Tantalus, who stood in a lake that reached his chin; he was dying to quench his thirst, but could never reach the water, for whenever the poor creature stooped to drink, it dried up and vanished, so that there was nothing but dry ground—parched by the spite of heaven. There were tall trees, moreover, that shed their fruit over his head—pears, pomegranates, apples, sweet figs and juicy olives, but whenever the poor creature stretched out his hand to take some, the wind tossed the branches back again to the clouds.[5]

Stygian Gloom

Awful, sombre, dismal.

The Styx was the river that separated the world of the living from the world of the dead, Hades. The ferryman Charon would transport the souls of the dead by way of this river into the Underworld. It was by the river Styx that the Greek gods swore their oaths, because, as a deity, she had sided with Zeus in the battle of the gods against the Titans, and was the first in springing to his aid. The Styx conferred invulnerability, too, as to Achilles, whose mother had dipped him into these waters as an infant. In doing so, she held him by one heel, which remained vulnerable, and he died in the Trojan War, pierced there by Paris' arrow.

Drinking from
the Waters of Lethe

To be in a state of oblivion.

Lethe [Λήθη] was one of the five rivers of
Hades, which flowed round the cave of
Hypnos ('sleep') and through the Underworld. All who drank from it forgot everything. The Greek word for truth, *αλήθεια*,
with the privative 'α', literally means 'un-
forgetfulness'. It is worth quoting here a
passage from the poem 'Letters of the Un-
living', by Mina Loy:

O leave me
my final illiteracy
of memory's languor

my preference
to drift in lenient coma
an older Ophelia
on Lethe.

Heroes

'Hero' is a Homeric word for rulers
or warriors of an exceptional stature.
Ideally, they are paragons of courage
and splendour. They are seen as
enjoying the favour of the gods
but need to act responsibly and
show initiative in dealing with
their tasks, which often have
a supernatural aspect.

Bellerophonic Letter

*A message maligning its bearer
or intended to cause him harm.*

Bellerophon's greatest feat was killing the Chimera, with the help of the winged horse Pegasus. When Bellerophon rejected the advances of the wife of his host, Proteus, she falsely accused him of ravishing her. Proteus, bound by the law of hospitality not to harm his guest, instead sent Bellerophon to his father-in-law, Iobates, with a sealed letter that read: 'Pray remove the bearer from this world: he attempted to violate my wife, your daughter.' But Iobates had feasted with Bellerophon before reading the letter, so he, too, feared divine retribution should he murder a guest. Thus, he asked the hero to slay the Chimera, thinking that Bellerophon was bound to perish in the attempt.

Chimerical

Outlandish, fantastical.

The Chimera, born of Typhon and Echidna, thus a sibling of Cerberus and the Lernaean Hydra, was a fire-breathing monster, comprising parts of several animals. She was usually depicted as a three-headed creature, with the head and foreparts of a lion, the head and body of a goat arising from her back and the head and body of a serpent for a tail. The Chimera terrorised ancient Lycia and its environs in Asia Minor, from which Mount Chimaera derived its name. Lycia is thought today to refer to the area of fiery gas vents now called Yanartaş (in Turkish, 'flaming rocks') in southwest Turkey.

Galaxy

Large groupings of stars and planets across the universe.

'Galaxias' [γαλαξίας] is the Greek name for the Milky Way, the galaxy of which our solar system is a part, and stems from the word γάλα, meaning 'milk'. When Zeus put the infant Hercules, his son by the mortal woman Alcmene, to nurse at the breast of the sleeping Hera so that he could be nourished with godlike qualities, she awoke to find she was nursing an unknown baby and pushed him away. The stars that make up the distinctive shape of the Milky Way derive their name from the milk that spurted from Hera's breast as a result.

Herculean Labour

A demanding task.

Seeking to atone for killing his wife and children in a fit of madness, Hercules consulted the oracle at Delphi. He was instructed to spend twelve years serving Eurystheus, the Mycenaean king, who set him twelve labours to perform:

1. Slay the Nemean Lion.
2. Slay the Lernaean Hydra.
3. Capture the Ceryneian Hind.
4. Capture the Erymanthian Boar.
5. Clean the Augean stables in a single day.
6. Slay the Stymphalian Birds.
7. Capture the Cretan Bull.
8. Steal the Mares of Diomedes.
9. Obtain the girdle of Hippolyta, queen of the Amazons.
10. Obtain the cattle of the monster Geryon.
11. Steal the apples of the Hesperides.
12. Capture and bring back Cerberus.

Hydra-headed

Proliferating evils.

The second labour of Hercules was to kill the Lernaean Hydra, a nine-headed monster, sibling of Cerberus and the Chimera. Having found that when he cut off a head two new ones would emerge from the stump, Hercules turned to his nephew Iolaus for help. Iolaus proposed using a torch to cauterise the stumps, and so they finally killed her.

Hercules and Iolaus slaying the Hydra:
Detail from a red-figured clay vase, about 450–500 BCE,
Regional Archaeological Museum, Palermo.

To Clean the Augean Stables

*To clear away corruption; perform
a difficult and unpleasant task
long overdue.*

The stables of King Augeas of Elis housed a large herd of cattle and had not been cleaned for years. As his fifth labour was to clean them, Hercules diverted the course of two rivers, the Alpheus and the Peneus, so that they flowed through the stables and swept the filth away, all in one day.

Shirt of Nessus

*Destructive or expiatory
influence or force.*

The centaur Nessus ferried Deianeira, Hercules' second wife, across a river, and attempted to ravish her. Seeing this, Hercules shot an arrow at the centaur, its tip poisoned with the Hydra's blood. The centaur's dying words were to tell Deianeira that his blood was a philtre that would keep her husband true to her forever. Growing jealous of Iole, her rival, Deianeira smeared the centaur's blood on Hercules' lion-skin tunic. The poison consumed the hero's flesh, so he built a funeral pyre and immolated himself in it. As he died, he was taken up to Olympus by Zeus and feted by the gods for his heroic exploits.

Procrustean Bed

*Forceful or unnatural means
to impose conformity.*

The young Theseus journeyed by land from Troezen to Athens to claim his birthright as prince of Athens, son of King Aegeus. On his travels he encountered and defeated many enemies, the last of which was Procrustes, who would force his captives to fit an iron bed, either stretching those who were too short for it or amputating the legs of those who were too tall. By this method he tortured and robbed all passing travellers. Theseus forced him to submit to the same treatment, and thus Procrustes met his end.

Labyrinthine

*Maze-like; a place in which
it is easy to get lost.*

The Labyrinth at the palace of Knossos
in Crete was a maze designed and constructed by the inventor Daedalus to hold
the Minotaur, the shameful half-man,
half-bull offspring of King Minos's wife,
Pasiphaë, who had mated with a bull.
Daedalus fashioned the Labyrinth so in-
geniously that he was hard put to find his
way out once he had built it.

Ariadne's Thread

*Means or reasoning
for solving a puzzle.*

Ariadne, the daughter of King Minos of
Crete (son of Zeus) and of Queen Pasiphaë (daughter of Helios), was put in
charge of guarding the Labyrinth that held
the Minotaur. Having fallen in love with
the hero Theseus, she helped him defeat
the Minotaur and emerge victorious by
her gifts to him of a sword, to kill the
monster, and a ball of thread, to unwind
as he made his way into the Labyrinth so
as to be able to find his way out again.

Academy

*A place of higher learning,
a select group of the learned.*

The Akademia was a sanctuary and grove sacred to Athena in her eponymous city of Athens, on the banks of the river Kephissus. Its name commemorated Akademos who had preserved Athens from the ire of the Dioskouroi, the twins Kastor and Polydeuces, by revealing the whereabouts of Helen, when she, as a young girl, was abducted by Theseus—long before she married Menelaus or eloped with Paris, thus starting the Trojan War. The Dioskouroi had been in a pair of eggs that contained Helen and Clytemnestra as well, hatched by Leda after she was ravished by Zeus in the form of a swan. Plato's school of philosophy was in the Akademia precinct, thus 'academy' has come to denote institutions of higher learning.

Argonaut

*Adventurer on a risky quest for
something of great value.*

The Argonauts were a band of heroes who
accompanied Jason to Colchis, on his
quest to obtain the Golden Fleece, the
fleece of a golden, winged ram that would
prove Jason the rightful king of Iolcus in
Thessaly. Argonaut means '*Argo*-sailor',
from the ship *Argo*, named after Argus,
her shipwright.

Harpy

Rapacious person, especially a woman.

King Phineus of Thrace, had been granted the gift of prophecy by Zeus. But for using this power to betray what the future held to mankind, Zeus punished Phineus by blinding him and stranding him on an island with a spread of food that could never be enjoyed because the half-bird, half-woman Harpies would swoop down to snatch it from his hands and eat it themselves, or sully it with their droppings. When the Argonauts reached the island, they delivered Phineus from his plight. In gratitude for their help, Phineus guided them on how to navigate safely between the Clashing Rocks, on their way to Colchis.

Amazon

Warlike woman.

The Amazons were a tribe of women warriors. Tough and aggressive, they were brave and formidable fighters. Several Greek heroes encountered them, such as Hercules, Theseus, Achilles and the Argonauts. Here is the passage on the Amazons in Apollonius of Rhodes' *Argonautica*:

And they would have tarried there and have closed in battle with the Amazons, and would have fought not without bloodshed for the Amazons were not gentle foes and regarded not justice, those dwellers on the Doeantian plain; but grievous insolence and the works of Ares were all their care; for by race they were the daughters of Ares and the nymph Harmonia, who bore to Ares war-loving maids, wedded to him in the glens of the Acmonian wood had not the breezes of Argestes come again from Zeus; and with the wind they left the rounded beach, where the Themiscyreian

Amazons were arming for war. For they dwelt not gathered together in one city, but scattered over the land, parted into three tribes. In one part dwelt the Themiscyreians, over whom at that time Hippolyte reigned, in another the Lycastians, and in another the dart-throwing Chadesians. And the next day they sped on and at nightfall they reached the land of the Chalybes.[6]

Sphinx

Puzzling or mysterious person.

The Sphinx was a monster with a human head, a lion's body, and wings springing from her back. She guarded the entrance to Thebes, and asked a riddle of travellers that they would have to answer correctly to be allowed passage: 'Which creature has four legs in the morning, two legs at noon and three legs in the evening?' She killed and devoured those unable to answer. It was Oedipus who finally solved the Sphinx's riddle: 'Man, who crawls on all fours as a baby, walks on two feet as an adult, and uses a walking stick in old age.' The Sphinx then threw herself from her high rock and perished.

Oedipus Complex

In Freudian psychoanalysis, the unconscious sexual desire of children, especially boys, towards their parent of the opposite sex while shunning their parent of the same sex.

Oedipus was raised by adoptive parents, and unwittingly fulfilled a prophecy that he would kill his father and wed his mother. Unknowingly, he killed his father Laius, king of Thebes, after the two quarrelled at the juncture of three roads, and as a reward for liberating Thebes from the Sphinx, Oedipus was himself crowned king of Thebes and married the widowed queen Jocasta, his mother. On discovering who his actual parents were, Oedipus blinded himself with the golden pin of Jocasta, who had already hanged herself.

The Iliad & *The Odyssey*

A legendary war was fought between
the Greeks and the Trojans over the
abduction of the beautiful Helen, wife
of Menelaus, king of Sparta, by Paris,
prince of Troy. The travails of all the
distinguished heroes who took part
in it, and the Greeks' return home,
were sung by many ancient poets,
now forgotten. Homer's name,
however, has remained indelibly
linked to these narratives
across the millennia.

Apple of Discord

*Something that causes
strife or jealousy.*

In retaliation for not having been invited
to the wedding feast of Peleus and Thetis
(who were to become the parents of
Achilles), the goddess Eris ('strife') let fall
amidst the wedding guests her Golden
Apple of Discord, with the inscription,
'For the most beautiful'. This led to a dispute among Hera, Athena and Aphrodite
as to who was the most beautiful, which
they asked Paris, a son of King Priam of
Troy, to adjudicate. He awarded the apple
to Aphrodite, and the spurned goddesses
ensured that the city of Troy was destroyed
in the war that ensued. Thus, the expression 'apple of discord' signifies the gist of
an argument, or a minor issue that may
blow up into a major dispute.

Achilles' Heel

*Weak point, a chink in
one's defences.*

When Achilles was born, it was foretold
that he would die young. To avert his
death, his mother Thetis dipped him into
the water of the river Styx, which granted
invulnerability, but, as she gripped him by
his heel, that part of his body remained
vulnerable. Thus he died in the Trojan
War, his heel pierced by a poisonous arrow
shot by Paris.

Stentorian Voice

Powerful, booming voice.

Stentor was a herald of the Greeks. He gets a brief mention in the *Iliad* when Hera exhorts the Greeks to fight:

There Hera stood still and raised a shout like that of brazen-voiced Stentor, whose cry was as loud as that of fifty men together. 'Argives,' she cried; 'shame on you cowardly creatures, brave in semblance only!'[7]

Cassandra's Prophesies

*Correct predictions that fail
to gain credence.*

Cassandra, a daughter of the Trojan king Priam and queen Hecuba, was cursed to utter true prophecies that no one would believe. Apollo, in an effort to seduce her, had given her the gift of prophecy, but when she rejected him, he spat into her mouth making it so that no one would ever believe her words. She was raped by Ajax after Troy's fall and was then taken as a concubine by King Agamemnon of Mycenae, who brought her home with him. As Cassandra foretold, when they arrived, the king's wife Clytemnestra and her lover Aegisthus murdered them both.

Electra Complex

*A counterpart of the Oedipus complex
of sexual possessiveness towards one
parent and antagonism towards
the other, but as regards women.*

A chiefly Jungian psychoanalytic term and disputed by Freud, it describes a girl's sense of competition with her mother for the affections of her father. Electra with Orestes, her brother, avenged the murder of their father, Agamemnon, by killing his murderers: their mother, Clytemnestra, and Aegisthus, her paramour.

Palladium

*Something that bestows protection
or security, a safeguard.*

The word 'palladium' derives from the
wooden effigy of Pallas Athena that pro-
tected the city of Troy. For the city to fall,
the effigy needed first to be removed from
within the boundaries of the city, and was
stolen by Odysseus and Diomedes who
gained access to it by means of a secret
passage.

Trojan Horse

Ruse that offers a temptation to lower a target's defenses. A type of computer virus.

A giant hollow wooden horse on wheels, made at Odysseus's behest and left at the gates of Troy as a token of surrender. A force of Greeks hid inside it, however, and thus gained access to the city:

The Trojans themselves had drawn the horse into their fortress, and it stood there while they sat in council round it, and were in three minds as to what they should do. Some were for breaking it up then and there; others would have it dragged to the top of the rock on which the fortress stood, and then thrown down the precipice; while yet others were for letting it remain as an offering and propitiation for the gods. And this was how they settled it in the end, for the city was doomed when it took in that horse, within which were all the bravest of the Argives waiting to bring death and destruction on the Trojans.[8]

Lotus Eaters

*People wallowing in pleasure instead
of dealing with practical concerns.*

In Book IX of the *Odyssey*, Odysseus re-
counts that, just as they were rounding
Cape Malea, the southernmost tip of the
Peloponnese, so as to sail westwards towards Ithaca, north headwinds blew him
and his comrades off course:

We reached the land of the Lotus-eaters, who
live on a food that comes from a kind of
flower. The lotus was so delicious that those
who ate of it left off caring about home, and
did not even want to go back and say what
had happened to them, but were for staying
and munching lotus with the Lotus-eaters
without thinking further of their return; nevertheless, though they wept bitterly I forced
them back to the ships and made them fast
under the benches.[9]

Siren Song

Alluring and harmful.

With their enchanting singing voices, the Sirens—half human, half bird—enticed passing sailors so that their ships would be wrecked on the rocky coast of their island abode, and there the Sirens would tear the sailors to pieces. Curious as to what the Sirens' song sounded like, Odysseus had himself tied to the mast with rope while his sailors stopped their ears with wax. On hearing their singing, he beseeched his men to let him loose but they just pulled his knots tighter, only releasing him once they had passed out of earshot. The Sirens, however, were to die if anybody heard their singing and escaped them, thus after Odysseus had sailed by, they hurled themselves into the sea and perished.

Odysseus and the Sirens: Detail from a red-figured
stamnos, about 480–470 BCE, British Museum, London.

Between Scylla and Charybdis

Inescapable choice between two evils.

On their voyage home, Odysseus and his men sailed through the strait of Messina, a channel flanked by two sea monsters a mere arrow-shot apart: Charybdis, a shapeless creature that swallowed up and spewed out the sea thrice a day in a whirlpool that wrecked ships and drowned their crews; and, Scylla, with her six canine heads, lurking in the crags of a mist-shrouded rock face, snatching up sailors from vessels sailing past her and eating them alive. To avoid one meant sailing close to the other. However, Circe the sorceress had told Odysseus to keep to Scylla's side—better lose a few shipmates than have the entire ship perish.

Mentor

*One who gives good counsel and
assistance to the inexperienced
in an endeavour.*

Mentor was an old friend of Odysseus
whose guise the goddess Athena assumed
in order to advise Odysseus' son Tele-
machus, in his father's absence, as well as
to give guidance to Odysseus himself
towards the end of the *Odyssey*.

Faithful Argos

Utterly loyal.

Argos was Odysseus' dog. After ten years fighting in Troy, and another ten years journeying home, Odysseus finally arrives in Ithaca. Self-interested suitors had ensconced themselves in his house, vying for the hand of Penelope, his wife, in his absence. To pass unnoticed among them, Odysseus disguised himself as a beggar:

A dog that had been lying asleep raised his head and pricked up his ears. This was Argos, whom Odysseus had bred before setting out for Troy, but he had never had any work out of him. [...] As soon as he saw Odysseus standing there, he dropped his ears and wagged his tail, but he could not get close up to his master. When Odysseus saw the dog on the other side of the yard, he dashed a tear from his eyes without Eumaios seeing it, and said: 'Eumaeus, what a noble hound that is over there on the manure heap: his build is splendid; is he as fine a fellow as he looks, or is he only one of those dogs that come begging about a table, and are kept merely for show? 'This dog,' answered Eumaios, 'belonged to him who has died in a far country. If he were what he was when Odysseus left for Troy, he would soon show you what he could do. There was not a wild beast in the forest that could get away from him when he was once on its tracks. But now he has fallen on evil times, for his master is dead and gone, and the women take no care of him. Servants never do their work when their master's hand is no longer over them, for Zeus takes half the goodness out of a man when he makes a slave of him.' So saying he entered the well-built mansion, and made straight for the riotous pretenders in the hall. But Argos passed into the darkness of death, now that he had fulfilled his destiny of faith and seen his master once more after twenty years.[10]

Zeus wielding a thunderbolt in one hand
with an eagle perched on the other hand.
Detail of a red-figured amphora,
about 480–470 BCE, Louvre, Paris.

1. οὗ χεῖρες μὲν ἔασιν ἐπ᾽ ἰσχύι, ἔργματ᾽ ἔχουσαι,
   καὶ πόδες ἀκάματοι κρατεροῦ θεοῦ· ἐκ δέ οἱ ὤμων
   ἦν ἑκατὸν κεφαλαὶ ὄφιος, δεινοῖο δράκοντος,
   γλώσσησιν δνοφερῇσι λελιχμότες, ἐκ δέ οἱ ὄσσων
   θεσπεσίης κεφαλῇσιν ὑπ᾽ ὀφρύσι πῦρ ἀμάρυσσεν·
   [πασέων δ᾽ ἐκ κεφαλέων πῦρ καίετο δερκομένοιο·]
   φωναὶ δ᾽ ἐν πάσῃσιν ἔσαν δεινῇς κεφαλῇσι
   παντοίην ὄπ᾽ ἰεῖσαι ἀθέσφατον· ἄλλοτε μὲν γὰρ
   φθέγγονθ᾽ ὥστε θεοῖσι συνιέμεν, ἄλλοτε δ᾽ αὖτε
   ταύρου ἐριβρύχεω, μένος ἀσχέτου, ὄσσαν ἀγαύρου,
   ἄλλοτε δ᾽ αὖτε λέοντος ἀναιδέα θυμὸν ἔχοντος,
   ἄλλοτε δ᾽ αὖ σκυλάκεσσιν ἐοικότα, θαύματ᾽ ἀκοῦσαι,
   ἄλλοτε δ᾽ αὖ ῥοίζεσχ᾽, ὑπὸ δ᾽ ἤχεεν οὔρεα μακρά.

   [Hesiod, *Theogony* 823–835,
   trans. H.G. Evelyn-White]

2. γεννᾶσθαι τὴν τοῦ σώματος φύσιν ἔχοντα μεμιγμέ-
   νην ἐξ ἀνδρὸς καὶ γυναικός· καὶ τὴν μὲν εὐπρέπειαν
   καὶ μαλακότητα τοῦ σώματος ἔχειν γυναικὶ παρεμ-
   φερῆ, τὸ δ᾽ ἀρρενωπὸν καὶ δραστικὸν ἀνδρὸς ἔχειν
   τὰ δὲ φυσικὰ μόρια συγγεννᾶσθαι τούτῳ καὶ γυ-
   ναικὸς καὶ ἀνδρός· ἔνιοι δὲ τὰ τοιαῦτα γένη ταῖς φύ-
   σεσιν ἀποφαίνονται τέρατα ὑπάρχειν, καὶ γεννώμενα
   σπανίως προσημαντικὰ γίνεσθαι ποτὲ μὲν κακῶν
   ποτὲ δ᾽ ἀγαθῶν.

   [Diodorus Siculus, *Bibliotheca Historica*, 4.6,
   trans. C.H. Oldfather]

3. καὶ γάρ τ᾽ ἠΰκομος Νιόβη ἐμνήσατο σίτου,
   τῇ περ δώδεκα παῖδες ἐνὶ μεγάροισιν ὄλοντο
   ἓξ μὲν θυγατέρες, ἓξ δ᾽ υἱέες ἡβώοντες.
   τοὺς μὲν Ἀπόλλων πέφνεν ἀπ᾽ ἀργυρέοιο βιοῖο
   χωόμενος Νιόβῃ, τὰς δ᾽ Ἄρτεμις ἰοχέαιρα,
   οὕνεκ᾽ ἄρα Λητοῖ ἰσάσκετο καλλιπαρῄῳ·
   φῆ δοιὼ τεκέειν, ἣ δ᾽ αὐτὴ γείνατο πολλούς·
   τὼ δ᾽ ἄρα καὶ δοιώ περ ἐόντ᾽ ἀπὸ πάντας ὄλεσσαν.
   οἳ μὲν ἄρ᾽ ἐννῆμαρ κέατ᾽ ἐν φόνῳ, οὐδέ τις ἦεν
   κατθάψαι, λαοὺς δὲ λίθους ποίησε Κρονίων·
   τοὺς δ᾽ ἄρα τῇ δεκάτῃ θάψαν θεοὶ Οὐρανίωνες.
   ἣ δ᾽ ἄρα σίτου μνήσατ᾽, ἐπεὶ κάμε δάκρυ χέουσα.
   νῦν δέ που ἐν πέτρῃσιν ἐν οὔρεσιν οἰοπόλοισιν
   ἐν Σιπύλῳ, ὅθι φασὶ θεάων ἔμμεναι εὐνὰς
   νυμφάων, αἵ τ᾽ ἀμφ᾽ Ἀχελώϊον ἐρρώσαντο,
   ἔνθα λίθος περ ἐοῦσα θεῶν ἐκ κήδεα πέσσει.

[Homer, *The Iliad*, XXIV, 603–618,
all translations from Homer by Samuel Butler]

4. καὶ μὴν Σίσυφον εἰσεῖδον κρατέρ᾽ ἄλγε᾽ ἔχοντα
   λᾶαν βαστάζοντα πελώριον ἀμφοτέρῃσιν.
   ἦ τοι ὁ μὲν σκηριπτόμενος χερσίν τε ποσίν τε
   λᾶαν ἄνω ὤθεσκε ποτὶ λόφον· ἀλλ᾽ ὅτε μέλλοι
   ἄκρον ὑπερβαλέειν, τότ᾽ ἀποστρέψασκε κραταιίς·
   αὖτις ἔπειτα πέδονδε κυλίνδετο λᾶας ἀναιδής.
   αὐτὰρ ὅ γ᾽ ἂψ ὤσασκε τιταινόμενος, κατὰ
   δ᾽ ἱδρὼς ἔρρεεν ἐκ μελέων, κονίη δ᾽ ἐκ κρατὸς ὀρώρει.

[Homer, *The Odyssey*, XI, 593–598]

5. καὶ μὴν Τάνταλον εἰσεῖδον κρατέρ᾽ ἄλγε᾽ ἔχοντα
   ἑστεῶτ᾽ ἐν λίμνη: ἡ δὲ προσέπλαζε γενείῳ:
   στεῦτο δὲ διψάων, πιέειν δ᾽ οὐκ εἶχεν ἑλέσθαι:
   ὁσσάκι γὰρ κύψει᾽ ὁ γέρων πιέειν μενεαίνων,
   τοσσάχ᾽ ὕδωρ ἀπολέσκετ᾽ ἀναβροχέν, ἀμφὶ δὲ ποσσὶ
   γαῖα μέλαινα φάνεσκε, καταζήνασκε δὲ δαίμων.
   δένδρεα δ᾽ ὑψιπέτηλα κατὰ κρῆθεν χέε καρπόν,
   ὄγχναι καὶ ῥοιαὶ καὶ μηλέαι ἀγλαόκαρποι
   συκέαι τε γλυκεραὶ καὶ ἐλαῖαι τηλεθόωσαι:
   τῶν ὁπότ᾽ ἰθύσει᾽ ὁ γέρων ἐπὶ χερσὶ μάσασθαι,
   τὰς δ᾽ ἄνεμος ῥίπτασκε ποτὶ νέφεα σκιόεντα.

   [Homer, *The Odyssey*, XI, 582–592]

6. καί νύ κε δηθύνοντες Ἀμαζονίδεσσιν ἔμιξαν
   ὑσμίνην, καὶ δ᾽ οὔ κεν ἀναιμωτί γ᾽ ἐρίδηναν—
   οὐ γὰρ Ἀμαζονίδες μάλ᾽ ἐπήτιδες, οὐδὲ θέμιστας
   τίουσαι πεδίον Δοιάντιον ἀμφενέμοντο:
   ἀλλ᾽ ὕβρις στονόεσσα καὶ Ἄρεος ἔργα μεμήλει:
   δὴ γὰρ καὶ γενεὴν ἔσαν Ἄρεος Ἁρμονίης τε
   νύμφης, ἥ τ᾽ Ἄρηϊ φιλοπτολέμους τέκε κούρας,
   ἄλσεος Ἀκμονίοιο κατὰ πτύχας εὐνηθεῖσα—
   εἰ μὴ ἄρ᾽ ἐκ Διόθεν πνοιαὶ πάλιν Ἀργέσταο
   ἤλυθον: οἱ δ᾽ ἀνέμῳ περιηγέα κάλλιπον ἀκτήν,
   ἔνθα Θεμισκύρειαι Ἀμαζόνες ὡπλίζοντο.
   οὐ γὰρ ὁμηγερέες μίαν ἂμ πόλιν, ἀλλ᾽ ἀνὰ γαῖαν
   κεκριμέναι κατὰ φῦλα διάτριχα ναιετάασκον:
   νόσφι μὲν αἵδ᾽ αὐταί, τῇσιν τότε κοιρανέεσκεν
   Ἱππολύτη, νόσφιν δὲ Λυκάστιαι ἀμφενέμοντο,

νόσφι δ᾽ ἀκοντοβόλοι Χαδήσιαι. ἤματι δ᾽ ἄλλῳ
νυκτί τ᾽ ἐπιπλομένῃ Χαλύβων παρὰ γαῖαν ἵκοντο.

[Apollonius Rhodius, *Argonautica*, II, 985–1001,
trans. R.C. Seaton]

7. ἔνθα στᾶσ᾽ ἤϋσε θεὰ λευκώλενος Ἥρη
Στέντορι εἰσαμένη μεγαλήτορι χαλκεοφώνῳ,
ὃς τόσον αὐδήσασχ᾽ ὅσον ἄλλοι πεντήκοντα:
αἰδὼς Ἀργεῖοι κάκ᾽ ἐλέγχεα εἶδος ἀγητοί.

[Homer, *The Iliad*, V, 785–788]

8. εἴατ᾽ ἐνὶ Τρώων ἀγορῇ κεκαλυμμένοι ἵππῳ·
αὐτοὶ γάρ μιν Τρῶες ἐς ἀκρόπολιν ἐρύσαντο.
ὣς ὁ μὲν ἑστήκει, τοὶ δ᾽ ἄκριτα πόλλ᾽ ἀγόρευον
ἥμενοι ἀμφ᾽ αὐτόν· τρίχα δέ σφισιν ἥνδανε βουλή,
ἠὲ διατμῆξαι κοῖλον δόρυ νηλέϊ χαλκῷ,
ἢ κατὰ πετράων βαλέειν ἐρύσαντας ἐπ᾽ ἄκρης,
ἢ ἐάαν μέγ᾽ ἄγαλμα θεῶν θελκτήριον εἶναι,
τῇ περ δὴ καὶ ἔπειτα τελευτήσεσθαι ἔμελλεν·
αἶσα γὰρ ἦν ἀπολέσθαι, ἐπὴν πόλις ἀμφικαλύψῃ
δουράτεον μέγαν ἵππον, ὅθ᾽ εἴατο πάντες ἄριστοι
Ἀργεῖοι Τρώεσσι φόνον καὶ κῆρα φέροντες.

[Homer, *The Odyssey*, XIII, 503–513]

9. ἐπέβημεν
γαίης Λωτοφάγων, οἵ τ᾽ ἄνθινον εἶδαρ ἔδουσιν ...
τῶν δ᾽ ὅς τις λωτοῖο φάγοι μελιηδέα καρπόν,
οὐκέτ᾽ ἀπαγγεῖλαι πάλιν ἤθελεν οὐδὲ νέεσθαι,
ἀλλ᾽ αὐτοῦ βούλοντο μετ᾽ ἀνδράσι Λωτοφάγοισι

λωτὸν ἐρεπτόμενοι μενέμεν νόστου τε λαθέσθαι.
τοὺς μὲν ἐγὼν ἐπὶ νῆας ἄγον κλαίοντας ἀνάγκῃ,
νηυσὶ δ᾽ ἐνὶ γλαφυρῇσιν ὑπὸ ζυγὰ δῆσα ἐρύσσας.

[Homer, *The Odyssey*, IX, 83–84, 94–99]

10. ἂν δὲ κύων κεφαλήν τε καὶ οὔατα κείμενος ἔσχεν,
Ἄργος, Ὀδυσσῆος ταλασίφρονος, ὅν ῥά ποτ᾽ αὐτὸς
θρέψε μέν, οὐδ᾽ ἀπόνητο, πάρος δ᾽ εἰς Ἴλιον ἱρὴν
ᾤχετο. […] ὡς ἐνόησεν Ὀδυσσέα ἐγγὺς ἐόντα,
οὐρῇ μέν ῥ᾽ ὅ γ᾽ ἔσηνε καὶ οὔατα κάββαλεν ἄμφω,
ἆσσον δ᾽ οὐκέτ᾽ ἔπειτα δυνήσατο οἷο ἄνακτος
ἐλθέμεν: αὐτὰρ ὁ νόσφιν ἰδὼν ἀπομόρξατο δάκρυ,
ῥεῖα λαθὼν Εὔμαιον, ἄφαρ δ᾽ ἐρεείνετο μύθῳ:
«Εὔμαι᾽, ἦ μάλα θαῦμα, κύων ὅδε κεῖτ᾽ ἐνὶ κόπρῳ.
καλὸς μὲν δέμας ἐστίν, ἀτὰρ τόδε γ᾽ οὐ σάφα οἶδα,
εἰ δὴ καὶ ταχὺς ἔσκε θέειν ἐπὶ εἴδεϊ τῷδε,
ἦ αὔτως οἷοί τε τραπεζῆες κύνες ἀνδρῶν
γίγνοντ᾽: ἀγλαΐης δ᾽ ἕνεκεν κομέουσιν ἄνακτες.»
τὸν δ᾽ ἀπαμειβόμενος προσέφης, Εὔμαιε συβῶτα:
«καὶ λίην ἀνδρός γε κύων ὅδε τῆλε θανόντος.
εἰ τοιόσδ᾽ εἴη ἠμὲν δέμας ἠδὲ καὶ ἔργα,
οἷόν μιν Τροίηνδε κιὼν κατέλειπεν Ὀδυσσεύς,
αἶψά κε θηήσαιο ἰδὼν ταχυτῆτα καὶ ἀλκήν.
οὐ μὲν γάρ τι φύγεσκε βαθείης βένθεσιν ὕλης
κνώδαλον, ὅττι δίοιτο: καὶ ἴχνεσι γὰρ περιῄδη:
νῦν δ᾽ ἔχεται κακότητι, ἄναξ δέ οἱ ἄλλοθι πάτρης
ὤλετο, τὸν δὲ γυναῖκες ἀκηδέες οὐ κομέουσι.
δμῶες δ᾽, εὖτ᾽ ἂν μηκέτ᾽ ἐπικρατέωσιν ἄνακτες,

οὐκέτ᾽ ἔπειτ᾽ ἐθέλουσιν ἐναίσιμα ἐργάζεσθαι·
ἥμισυ γάρ τ᾽ ἀρετῆς ἀποαίνυται εὐρύοπα Ζεὺς
ἀνέρος, εὖτ᾽ ἄν μιν κατὰ δούλιον ἦμαρ ἕλησιν.»
ὣς εἰπὼν εἰσῆλθε δόμους εὖ ναιετάοντας,
βῆ δ᾽ ἰθὺς μεγάροιο μετὰ μνηστῆρας ἀγαυούς.
Ἄργον δ᾽ αὖ κατὰ μοῖρ᾽ ἔλαβεν μέλανος θανάτοιο,
αὐτίκ᾽ ἰδόντ᾽ Ὀδυσσῆα ἐεικοστῷ ἐνιαυτῷ.

[Homer, *The Odyssey*, XVII, 291–328]

Index of Entries

General Index

AN ANTHOLOGY

Words of Wisdom
from Ancient Greece

Translated by Alexander Zaphiriou
Illustrated by Panagiotis Stavropoulos

BILINGUAL EDITION

Words of Wisdom from Ancient Greece gathers the
best of a thousand years of philosophy, history and
literature, in a compilation of writing spanning from
800 BCE to 200 AD. This survey of ancient wisdom
offers guidance for a life well lived from luminaries of
Greece's legendary past.

EPICTETUS

Manual
on the Art of Living

Translated by P.E. Matheson

BILINGUAL EDITION

'Of all existing things, some are in our power, and others are not in our power.' So begins the *Manual* or *Enchiridion* of Epictetus, a collection of precepts that together provide a powerful philosophy for daily life. The *Manual*, considered to be the pinnacle of Stoic philosophy, addresses living with integrity, self-management and personal freedom.

PYTHAGORAS

The Golden Verses

Translated by David Connolly

BILINGUAL EDITION

The essence of Pythagoras' teachings is contained in *The Golden Verses*, seventy-one verses as guidelines on how to live. Functioning as admonitions, they link the human with the divine element and determine the point at which both elements converge to reveal how we might ourselves attain this supreme virtue in our everyday lives.

HIPPOCRATES

Aphorisms

Translated by W.H.S. Jones

BILINGUAL EDITION

Hippocrates of Kos, often referred to as the 'Father of Western Medicine', is credited with being the first healer to separate the discipline of medicine from religion, arguing that disease was not a punishment inflicted by the gods but rather the product of environmental factors, diet and lifestyle. *Aphorisms*, the best known work in the whole *Hippocratic Corpus*, is a series of propositions concerning the symptoms and diagnosis of disease and medicine, and the art of healing. The tradition is that Hippocrates composed it in his old age as a summary of his vast experience.